Analfabeto / An Alphabet

Chapbooks by Ellen Baxt:

Enumeration of colonies is not EPA approved.
The day is a ladle
Tender Chemistry
Since I Last Wrote

Analfabeto / An Alphabet

ELLEN BAXT

Shearsman Books
Exeter

Published in the United Kingdom in 2007 by
Shearsman Books Ltd
58 Velwell Road
Exeter EX4 4LD

www.shearsman.com

ISBN-13   978-1-905700-36-3

ISBN-10   1-905700-36-9

ARTS COUNCIL
ENGLAND

The publisher gratefully acknowledges financial assistance from
Arts Council England.

Analfabeto

An Alphabet

For Fay Baxt Cohen, 1907-1998
My first storyteller
Her hands were soft, a good time for breathing

Everyone wears white. Everyone orders something that
sizzles. There is a deep voice speaking a sound check into
a microphone. Um dois tres. Dois tres. Um dois. Um um.

The concert hall is a shell. The couples in love are hot and testy.
The dishes are for two. I waste half.

The couples sit next to each other or
The couples sit side by side.

Crossing the street, the mother drags on a cigarette. The mother drags her son across the street. Across the street, the mother is in spandex drag but is a woman. Her son sucks his white pacifier.

Outside City Hall there is a banner that says Agora Justiça and Engenho da Mata. There is a big red X through the words Estados Unidos. The post office is always closed or seen from a bus window. On Sundays the street at Copacabana is closed to cars and the tan bicyclists ride by. The boys want to know what I'm writing.

Analfabeto	Illiterate
	affection or
	disease
	Easter lily
	I have to set my watch.
	They went up the street. Dawn.
	Let me light a match. target,
	aim or white: swallow
	We have no firearms.
	to long for, an appetite
	Let's go out in the open air.
	We're going to clip his wings.
	Everything's fine. Blue

A motorcycle delivers blue cylinders of water.

The buildings have two addresses, one above the other so
you are always at the wrong building.

Pressure of proximity.

The boy does not want to enter the church. There are witches.
Also there are Catholic saints in African melodies.

The American woman on the beach is barbudo, heavily bearded on her legs. When the children whisper bigode, mustache, she pretends not to understand, but stiff shoulders. On the plaza a girl asks, You are a fabiana? but she doesn't know fabiana. You are like my friend, she says. If the friend's husband finds out, finger slices neck, but on the plaza they are on laps. A hand reaches up and takes a breast. Another reaches down between thighs. Mamão is papaya. Mamãe is mommy. Mamar is to suck or milk.

Fabio is from Rio and tells me I must not go alone to Caruaru. Having found me at the train station, he taps my shoulder. Reclining in our reclining chairs he asks if I am sad. No, I just like watching Brazil out the window. You have beautiful eyes. You have a boyfriend? No, I am a lesbian. I not can kiss you then? No, you not can kiss me. In Brazil it is not good to be like you, but one day your people will have their day of glory.

There are many stars above Salvador. My mother is bowling in her blue bowling bracelet.

Humidity curls the pages. Sometimes I lie about sozinha/solteira. Because it is New Year's Eve, the avó in the elevator wishes me saúde, prosperidade e bom marido.

Só is only. Sozinha is alone.

A person should drink two liters of water a day. Eu tenho saudade. People should stand behind the yellow line. My city is clean. I have one sister and one brother. I stay hungry. The president won on a three-meal-a-day platform. On TV, O Brasil que come ajudando o Brasil que tem fome with the Brazilian flag as a tablecloth. A yellow-vested waiter serves a patron from a platter, fork and spoon in one hand like tongs. A woman chirps Tudo bem? into her phone. Tudo.

When I am writing on the plaza suddenly there is a circle of children. Write my name. Write my name. Write my name.
LETICIA
GABRIELA
LUÁ
LUIZ ANDRÉ
JOÃO VICTOR
Write your name. ELLEN
Say something in English. Say something in Spanish. A dog is chewing an itch. What can you write? A flatbed truck carrying petroleum. The museum is closed. The dog leaves. At the bookstore café there is: ler   ouvir   comer. Read hear eat. I am not so afraid in Niterói. There are one-storey houses and a cluster of men playing guitar and singing. Guitar is violão. The wind is picking up. A plane lands over the water as the ferry departs. Christine is at her desk in the Palisades plotting Grimano, Italy. The kids stand up and pump their swings. Intermittently, a bell rings. Across the water they're trying to get rid of the winter clothes. The mannequins' shirts say "Liquidação" across their torpedoed breasts.

My hair's getting long. I miss my brother and the red carpeting in the hall. I told them I'm going to stay. Unexpectedly, I found a career.

1. Choose
2. Shoes

1. Batch
2. Badge

1. Pin
2. Pen

Outside the movie theater I buy caramel popcorn in a brown bag. She buys pão doce with coconut shreds. *Lisbela e o Prisioneiro* is a comedy and sometimes I laugh at the right times. She thinks it is only in Brazil that people talk during the movies and complains about her people's manners, falta da educação. In the dark she puts on her glasses. Later she shows me where to buy shirts and pants and underpants. I blush.

They up the street went walking watch setting. Tomorrow another day is very. Pipoca is the edge of carnaval. Pleasing to meet you. You will ring my finger? You will house with me? Please elect another option from the menu. Bread and lilies will be distributed en route. Turn me a match on fire. Say me the difference, hurt and heart.

My right ovary wakes me at 1 am, wanting to discuss yesterday's lesson, what I'll say in class, and a general critique of how things are going at this particular juncture. Yesterday the esfiha de frango was orange inside. What I thought was celery turned out to be cartilage. The suco de melão was light and the suco de pêssego was hearty. My right ovary is singing and somewhat off key.

Dear A,
I miss dressing quietly with you asleep on the edge of the bed.
I miss your neck.
I miss the shape of your fingernails
and the size of your palms.
Inhale. As you exhale, release the muscle around the outer hip.
Inhale, the back expands and fills with light. I miss my body.

Phonics means that grapes is not grasps or gasps or grates or graze. When teaching the word lasts, make the sound of cymbals. Compromisso is appointment; oficina, garage; sensível, sensitive. The Botanic Garden is fifty-four hectares. Being unshaven at the beach, I call attention to the act of shaving, though the act of shaving is what I haven't done. A fruit is fuzzy but an animal is furry. An orange has a rind; a tomato, a skin; a banana, a peel. We eat cucumber seeds but not watermelon seeds. In Hortifruti, cantaloupe is melão americano. When I write I think I've made a noise. Looking up, the quiet is startling.

assets, goods or belongings

result or

consequence; The words had a bad effect,

axle or axis

They're going to build a new school. She

She doesn't know anything. Elasticity

Who headed the revolution?

pledge   pawning   obligation

joiner (masculine)

penetrate or

soak. Send me a dozen.   delivery

or surrender

They did it between the two of them. While

While we studied they wrote letters

ingenuity, wit

engenho   sugar mill

A man sings guitar up the cobblestones. Someone saws over head.
The sound, xaxado.

Ladies and Gentlemen, we are now beginning our descension
of Salvador.

The crossing guards are dressed as clowns because
people respect clowns.

Xaxado, danced in the inland deserts of the Northeast, is named for the sound of the farmers' sandals slapping against the dusty ground, sha-sha'doo. Both ends of the zabumba are hit with a stick or a light branch.

Êle tinha o hábito de levantar-se cedo.
Hálito. Hera.
Hidroavião. Hidrofobia.
Que horas são? São duas horas e meia.
A que horas começa a festa?
Está no hora da jantar. Hora de verão.
Horta. (feminina)

This is the month of the bus stop.
Concave, efficient
periphery sharpening like salt
but always. Ears scour behind. Slow and step aside
when footsteps or rustling.

      :Fuchsia lipstick. Big face.
      :Black?
      :No, tall. Very white.
      :Not Black?
      :This close, only lips. Five fingers around.
        A transvestite maybe.

A dog with eleven udders. I remember. A boy with spots of fur
on his arms asks Do I have many friends. The Frenchwoman says,
"We eat now. I'm angry." Soap gently and look away.
The mosquitoes make a funnel above.

This noise is heavily bearded. Children, that's too much blessing. A whale or a butterfly. Life is a beach.

Beautiful cake, let me bless you, stroke of a short while.

Heavily, the bell.
Badalada badalada badalada

or

Você é linda. Here is my telephone. I work at the restaurant on this picture preparing juices. You would like a cookie? You would like a cigarette? You will wait here. I will wash my sunglasses in the ocean. I don't live far. You will come to my room?

It is embarrassing to smell bad so there are three four five showers a day. It is not embarrassing to be a little chubby. It is embarrassing to miss dance class because I am afraid of the dark in the blackout when a lady is screaming in high heels running. Near Parque Treze de Maio and all the parks and bus stops and tailors and bakeries and newsstands there is a blackout. The lights brown, hum, then apagó! a woman is screaming. In the dark, the ball of her epiglottis trembles. Her scream comes closer, then backs away. It has a trill, like a flute. I stand too close to a man and his girlfriend who look up and ask what I want. I stand next to twin police officers because they have guns. Today I don't get mugged and I am not threatened with a gun. I also don't dance ciranda in the room with the wide wood planks and a mural of the poet Manuel Bandeira or flirt with the dark Italian. Skirt billow.

fada	fairy (feminine)
fado	fate or destiny (masculine)
	We must excuse his faults.
	need or lack, absence, fault or
	defect, mistake
	The ship leaks.
	Speak more slowly.
	You are
	the happiest day of my life.
	wild beast, play hooky, stay

fura   fury or fit

                            of madness (feminine)

                            They make good bread here.

                            hurricane (masculine)

                                        To frank (letters)

                                        grant passage

                                        open, to clear

                                        away (obstacles)

fica   stay

Fica com o troco.   Keep the change.

Chubby sings along to the radio. The pair carry their beach chairs into the shallow water. The transvestite has trouble lighting her cigarette in all this wind. Hair gloms to her lipstick. The ocean delays the sound of the pandeiro. The pandeiro arrives late. Sticks of cheese and bowls of fire. The peanuts that grow in the sea are mimona. The peanuts in the pink paper cones are handled by the boys' dirty hands. Wilem Doglas is ten and can say amendoim in six languages: Italian, Japanese, Spanish, French, Portuguese and now English.

My father sends me a poem he has written about sunset.

The Brazilian speaking English says it was beautiful but unacceptable, or the music refracts the English of the Brazilian. She says, When I was ten I broke my slack, pointing to her jaw. There was a car crash. She had to stay eating soup for 40 days.

The chairs and the bookcases are newly stained. In a small conspiracy against permanence, I cannot master local calling cards, only international ones. On the card, a picture of aqueducts. On the application, Do you dominate English?

In the North, cowboys in leather cowboy hats. It's not raining anymore, but the umbrellas haven't come down yet. Rio has many flowered umbrellas. A sentence begins with For example. In Portuguese, the answer is a verb. The filmmakers have had their carrot soup and will have the salmon next.

Both hands
snapping
means very.

Come by
the house
means we'll
see each
other again,
but is not
an invitation
to come by
the house.

Rua dos Judeus became Rua Bom Jesus. Blue script on white tile.

In 1654, a band of twenty-three Jews expelled by the Portuguese from Recife, Brazil, landed in the Dutch colony of New Amsterdam. From that day to the present, there has been a permanent Jewish population in what is now the United States.

In the vegetarian restaurant, paintings of cashew fruit with Hebrew signs. It smells like a Hari Krishna cafeteria, vinegar and shredded beets. Rua Bom Jesus is expensive. The synagogue is a museum. The sanctuary is closed except for special occasions. A stone well was found underground, mikva. You can read the list of names.

Silent consonants, pointing to history and kinship, are worth keeping.

H

He was in the habit

Breath

of getting up early.

Seaplane or flying-boat

hydrophobe or rabies   She hesitated in

What time is it?

vegetable garden

to drain

equine, of horses

They sugar mill between the two of them. Affections, heart and love don't penetrate glimmer. Surrender sugar. While entrails glisten, send me a dozen. She doesn't know belongings. She builds anything: persistence, elasticity, innermost parts. The words had an axle, an ask. You may soak joiner to go deeper into tissue. Soak had a bad effect. Who headed the revolution? The words, masculine: surrender and delivery. They did it while ingenuity built a new school. A new school doesn't know anything. Obligation drives between the two of them. Revolution studied while we wrote letters. Elasticity

Send me a dozen.

A hilltop room, Our Lady of Conceição/Oxum. I back away from a pair of transvestites like bears, slowly and without turning around. An old woman faints – the weight of the hoop skirt or, the spirit mounted her. A watermelon was smashed open. Afterwards, all the people had one hand full of popcorn.

Stay, you must to stay the night. The bus doesn't pass. Goes only to Port of Hens, not the city. Do not worry. Tomorrow will return you. Tomorrow.

Afterwards, I wouldn't sit near the door – rush of wind on my neck. Still, some breezes were unavoidable.

The women's necks
The women's tan toes
The women's small hands
The women's bellies
The women's knees
The women's wrists

Bento Teixeira, author of *Prosopopéia*, the first literary work written in Brazil, was persecuted for Jewish practices, as was Branca Dias, the first educator of women in Brazil. Ms. Dias was accused by her own students of Judaisms, mentioning her customs of cleaning the house on Fridays, of not working on Saturdays, using that day to clean clothes, and of eating a special dinner on Fridays.

Outside the puppet museum, banners of fringed paper. A man in a floral print horse held up by suspenders. Ladeira da Misericordia, a steep incline to the cathedral plaza. Food stalls and shade in Venn diagrams.

The white chairs and the constellations are stacked. Tomorrow Mars will be the biggest it has been in 5,000 years. He asks if she minds the music. On TV, the drug dealers from Rio are taken away in a van, twelve dead. Gilberto Gil and Lula stand behind a bouquet of microphones. Lula is Pernambucano.

The Brazilian teenagers explain why they do not throw their cups in the trashcan. Because our government is corrupt. If yes, then the street remains dirty. It is not correct, but this is how it is in Brazil. Our language is polluted with English. Um self-service means you have to weigh your plate. Santa Teresa is winning. We would like to leave our country and go to America. In America, containers are easy to open, but vegetables are not fresh, we know.

The nun makes good bread in rage. We must excuse her wild
beast, playing hooky, fault or defect:

furacão, fogo, ferradura

I can open the ship slowly, grant hunger, fire, a feminine passage.
I can't grant bread or horseshoe. Or hurricane. Bread was
the happiest day of my life. Do not mistake happiest.
Fado da minha vida.

On Saturday, a small bus. Chickens thrown in through
the window. Soon, a wedding.

May I remain gratefully yours?

                    You may mob or crowd, heathen or pagan.

Grenade remains gratefully yours. Os meninos gastan tudo
em pouco tempo.

We need bud or shoot. We don't need an umbrella, we need stew.
Indifference marked the car.

The desk, which did not smell like oranges, was made from orange crates, 1908, Kansas City. The family Bible had a family tree on the first page. It was heavy and black, tall. I was afraid. An aunt's hair burned. Vertical swirl. Siblings on the edge of a boat.

At the end of Rua de São Bento is the Colegio Santa Gertrudes, the highest point in Olinda. It was home to Jews Gonçalo Dias, tailor; Luís Antunes, chemist, married to Maria Alvarez; Rui Gomes, goldsmith, father of Luís Antunes; and Maria de Faria, married to Francisco Cordeiro, who lived on his farm.

Later, a lock was installed.

The Jews of Recife did not have a synagogue, but demonstrated
their religious concerns in a letter to the rabbi of Salônica,
Haim Shabetai:

"should we pray for rain between the months of
Tishrei and Nissan as other Jews do, or should we adapt
our prayers to the seasons of Brazil?"

Today is the twenty-seventh day of rain. In Pombos, the bridges
disappear and three thousand are ilhados. The mayor has declared
a state of emergency. The water is up to the triangles of roofs.
People are rowing past trees.

On Rua de São Bento, "the water arrives every day," but when
I turn the torneira, a thinning stream, then acabó. For six days,
acabó, while water leaks out the building onto the sidewalk.
A boy filling the hole with stones does not re-route the water to
apartamento cuatro.

The river and the bottom third of the riverstilts are green-black
Thick layer of rainbow. On the bridge
blue crabs in a pile
The little wooden baubles
clink, weaving a net for repair
A turn-of-the-century building is under
construction. Soon, a hotel – fans, strolling
An ad for Frevo Cola hangs the length of the building   I use it
facing North

impulse

momentum

beardless or young

violence or

fury, laborious

içar   To hoist the flag.

irmã   sister, magnet

                    Independence or

                    disinterestedness

                    cigarette lighter

In a small notebook, she keeps herself company in her own
language:

The bus driver knows all the children's names.
The lampshades are square baskets.
The party is always near the church.

The church hums with blue fluorescence. Flies crackle.
This toilet does not accept paper.
A bottle of beer blows a bubble that pops.

Guaraná has more caffeine than coffee.
The miniature carts produce miniature dixie cups
of thick espresso.

The beautiful women share a hammock and speak their
beautiful language. In their beautiful language, the
beautiful women share a hammock. The beautiful women
share a beautiful language, their hammock.

A boy in blue trunks goes for a midnight swim.
The backstage has wings. I fly.

Dear S,
The backstage has wings.
I fly,
E

Dear S,
I miss your pertinent.
Far is a longing.
E

Capibaribe River

dixie cups
condoms
#2 pencils
a phone card floating
the new museums create a posh sensibility but with prostitutes

fault or imperfection

hyacinth

The window in my room is large.

woman gardener or small table

a small bus

jet or stream, flash of light

boa constrictor (feminine)

jazida   Mineral deposit, bed or resting-place

fast or fasting

Jewelry store

Jesus Christ

It was a good play.

jubilation: rejoicing or retiring of

a teacher

judia   jewess

judiaria   ghetto

jaez   harness or trappings, kind or sort

jarreter   to hamstring, to cripple

Sieve or riddle

Woman with camisole crosses garden. The garden takes off her
camisole. You will undress me now. Drizzle.

Who takes care of the typesetting? studies tenement at university?

carroça carvalho chuvisco

Pebbles of dried meat, a shell, a small cup of black coffee. Sardine,
sanctuary. I will do caring with you, don't go already. Shell me in
our small cup.

Cart, masculine.
Who will scar? Who will drive the cart?

D. doesn't believe she has dengue fever
The wound molded over
making a smell like leather and ammonia in a dark place
Her elbow is obese. Next to the mattress
a watermelon and balanced on top
a serrated knife
I thought of how I might say, "your daughter is dying" in French
There was a high polyester count which made a shininess

Construction Materials

cardboard
black plastic
tin

newspaper
floral print
metal

tarp
thatch
bags

jagged bottle halves against the pigeons

Illiterate disease, we'll have to ring or link up the street together.

I have an appetite for going up the dawn. Clip my longing.

Let me land in the open air. A swallow, an Easter lily.

They corked his Everything's fine. The guards aimed with firearms.

Her friendship was on sale. I had to set my watch.

The window in my room is large. A sailing raft. Jet or stream.
Flash of light. Jubilação. A raft of light. A small flash of
jubilation. Tomorrow will very soon. The teacher retired his
window reading. The window is a retired teacher.

Judia. Judiaria. Jaez.

A small bus, a small table, a gardener. Hyacinth.
Masculine hyacinth is a good jewelry store. The day on its
knees. On donkey, it is June. In June, it was a good play.

Jarreter. Jumento.

Pour through the sieve. Grasp the mane. It is your move.

On the new year, fasting. Jazida.

Dinner riddle, come right now.

Because I understand the question, I am happy to answer
the woman in the red dress in a complete sentence, No, I do
not have fire. The boy in blue trunks is soft with quiet. The
nightclub is folkloric. I would like to stay.

Que quer dizer esta palavra? Divagação, wandering or digression.

Durable beam, her life was a difficult one. Pão duro. Dar a luz.
Desabrido. She is serrated, notched. She is durable, lasting.
She is, what does this word mean? Disguised, unequal. What is
the difference between unequal and unjust?

She does not have bread at her disposal. She has praise
in verse and song, liquids to learn by heart, sleeping to break in.

Speak slowly, you are a rough weather. You are to peck, to type.
You are sleeping beam at my disposal. We are apricot and damask.
We are to give birth. We are from the North, decorated by liquids.

She spreads her blanket over my geography, pushes the latch. At
dawn she asks if my family knows. In the van she covered our
legs and held my hand underneath. Você tem vontade? but I don't
know vontade.

Against:

Choose a photo from the album. She is very handsome. Upon meeting, the Brazilian asks the American, You believe in love at first sight? Later she asks, I ring your finger? She moved from São Paulo to Nossa Senhora de Ó. Before our first kiss, I cup her head. In the shower, she presses me. The tiles are cool against my skin vibrating.

N

This is quite natural.

ship or mist

To be born, to bed, rise

(sun) To originate.

No, neither fish nor fowl.

Our sister. Our town.

nape of the neck

daffodil or narcissist

daughter-in-law or water-wheel

novelty, news (item), crop (of fruit), strange

incident, mishap

to nourish or feed, to cherish

(hopes etc.)

Long means far. Near means pertinent.

Excuse me, may I use your fire? There is much wind.

You are very beautiful. With burning I will stay with you.

Eu perdí o ultimo ônibus means	I was distracted by your long lashes.
Fica comigo means	You will cover me with your small blanket.
Gostosa means	The feijão was delicious or your skin is very smooth.

Thank you for your wildcat dare. Yes, I have sheep, an ounce
of wave, a flap of a book. I have an oyster. Yesterday you were
shoulder, attention, declining sun. Thank you for your kindness.

I smell feminine glimpse, a milky egg. Show me to bone eight.
It is difficult to fall or Autumn, offering gold. Yesterday bore dew.
É difícil orientar-se nesta cidade.

setting (sun), decline

offering or gift

Thank you for your kindness.

shoulder, wave

Yesterday, ear or flap of a book

It's difficult to get one's bearings.

                                    Shade tree.

                                    Lemon.

                                    Milk.

            Autumn or Fall

            Yes, I have a watch.

            To dare

**Pouting means pushing the lips away from the teeth as if one
were pointing with one's mouth, forming a trumpet-shape.**

Mother

To suck or take the breast

Would you like something else?

Butter or flattery

Do it this way—

      the sea

      forest or woods ivory

      wick or fuse

      She is afraid.

Do you want wool or

cotton stockings?

Watermelon

Little girl, where do you live?

He's my best friend.

A long time ago

crutch (feminine)

handle or leaf

through a book

Hank or skein (of yarn). Intrigue.

Home-made remedy, moss.

Will you hold my arduous impulse? My rash is unscratchable.
You are my young magnet. Will you be my young magnet?
I will miss your bait or fried liver, your dishonest flag.

I miss my sister, notion of.
You want I braid your hair?
I miss my içar.

manga
mangaba

pêssego
goiaba

umbu
jambo

pera
morango

acerola
graviola

pinha
passa

abacaxí
abacati

guaraná
açaí

melão
limão

caju
caja

castanha
côco

com leite
sem leite

com gelo
sem gelo

Translation is not an equation. The equation is an asymptote. Oficina is garage, secretaria is desk, compromisso is appointment. In Brazil, you will teach in the morning and when you go to a friend's house for lunch, you will shower and nap, put your feet up. The roommate will talk about Barcelona and show you pictures. There are four straw fish on the wall.

I miss her. João Pessoa is the greenest city in the world.

The Casa da Cultura is a former slave prison which houses shops selling lace, leather and carved wooden handcrafts. Above each doorway is a sign with the name of the shop and below that, Cela and a number. Do you know what cela means? It is where the prisoner slaves were kept. The floor is stone. It is the only building that is cold. The bars have been painted lavender. The stairs are narrow and steep. You have to hold on. There is one cela that is left as it was, with rusted devices and springs.

At home, a man offers me limeade from a blender. A coffee filter has many uses.

Feminine is a scraped and close cropped fox. The watch is fast, reflex action. The brook is a trap, hard-fought and furious. Do you recognize this handwriting? Chubby, criminal, stern.

I admit, the frog is chubby as indicated.

When he heard the fox, he recognized this handwriting. Teeth were reduced to ashes under the tugboat. I will tugboat this reduce.

Be my student. You can triple the darkness. They all shiver translating it. They all say nap, portion, ankle. Do you blacken tune and air? There's no way to dishonest shiver. I know darkness.

                                                              tiger.
                                                    tuberculosis.
                                                                    .

The vowels

Howl.
That was the only time he spoke
to me.
Distinguished individual. Bear. Rude.
We're going to do everything possible
to unite them.

Look at this nostril. A noun is a scoundrel. Now I see.

Your candle wand measures 43.3 inches but chicken pox is both rustic and villainous. Smart and bright, I feel like curving into the long tomorrow.

Sailing meadow is crossing opportunity.

Sangrar	To bleed or drain
	soap, skirt
	To know by heart
	I'm homesick (for my
	country)
	salt and wit
Secar	To bleed, dry
	Dew. Open air.
	calm, clear or serene, arrow
	or hand (of a clock)
	cider, To have a sunbath
	parasol, to whisper
Só, sozinha	Only, alone
	Slant, sumptuous

On Rua General Gois Monteiro, I don't want to look at the dead bird on the sidewalk but I do anyway. I couldn't explain the difference between Look at and See, so I said they were the same. How can you ovulate on the right and shed on the left?

On the novela, a condom in its little square package like candy or a toy. The girl tells her mother that Rafaella is her girlfriend and the mother cries. A condom is a little T-shirt.

Beloved daughter.
A squadron. A gang. A square dance.
Problem, worry or jig-saw puzzle.
pre-Lenten

Sit next to me, orange treat. Flatter swiftly:

orange tree
lemon
milk

lilac
lemon tree
moon

When you're free, we'll talk.
We'll take by force.

The orange tree was taken by force. A feminine handwriting.
It won't free this translation. Smooth or even. Lavadeira: washing
machine or washerwoman. The washerwoman is milked.

She overcharged me, requiring that I bring blue powder soap,
bar soap and bleach which I did because she was a witch. Bony, a
look-away.

Sit next to me, blacklist flatterer. Slow my lion.

In French there is no word for saudade so D. approximates
sadness + nostalgia.

Bom dia, Sr. Silva. I am homesick for my country.
Heart is drain. Hand of a sunbath.
Sozinha. To have a parasol. To whisper.

Skirt, soap, saber de cor.

Alone, meaning both sumptuous and I'm homesick.
How do you say I am not married but I am parasol worshipper
in your country?
I bleed for my country, Sr. Silva, is not the same as
I bleed for Sr. Silva, my country.

Outside, a secret sunbath.

Acknowledgements

Excerpts from *Analfabeto / An Alphabet* have been published as chapbooks by Sona Books and Dusie, in the journals *XCP : Streetnotes*, *How2, spell* and *the tiny*.

Text is borrowed from *The Teaching of Pronunciation* by Peter MacCarthy and from the archive of Kahal Zur Israel, the first synagogue of the Americas, located in Recife, Brazil.

Thanks

Thank you to Jill Magi and Wayne Koestenbaum for multiple readings and thoughtful critique. Thank you to Sarah Leddy for frequent encouragement. Thank you to my students and teachers for offering language I could live in, including Lorna Goodison, Lorna McDaniel, Laura Hinton and Marty Skoble. Thank you to Tony Frazer for his patience, organization, and dedication to women's writing. And to those who have come before.